Netball Basics: How to Play Netball

ISBN-13: 978-1479117765

ISBN-10: 1479117765

Copyright Notice

All Rights Reserved © 2012 Kim Sundrey

This book is a work of the author's experience and opinion. This book is licensed for your personal enjoyment only. This book may not be re-sold or given away to other people. If you would like to share this book with another person please purchase an additional copy for each person you share it with. You may not distribute or sell this book or modify it in any way. The editorial arrangement, analysis, and professional commentary are subject to this copyright notice. No portion of this book may be copied, retransmitted, reposted, downloaded, decompiled, reverse engineered, duplicated, or otherwise used without the express written approval of the author, except by reviewers who may quote brief excerpts in connection with a review. The scanning, uploading and distribution of this book via the internet or via any other means without permission of the publisher is illegal and punishable by law. The publisher does not have any control over and does not assume any responsibility for author or third-party websites or their content. United States laws and regulations are public domain and not subject to copyright. Any unauthorized copying, reproduction, translation, or distribution of any part of this material without permission by the author is prohibited and against the law. Disclaimer and Terms of Use: No information contained in this book should be considered as financial, tax, or legal advice. Your reliance upon information and content obtained by you at or through this publication is solely at your own risk. The authors or publishers assume no liability or responsibility for damage or injury to you, other persons, or property arising from any use of any product, information, idea, or instruction contained in the content or services provided to you through this book. Reliance upon information contained in this material is solely at the reader's own risk. The authors have no financial interest in and receive no compensation from manufacturers of products or websites mentioned in this book. Whilst attempts have been made to verify information provided in this publication, neither the author nor the publisher assumes any responsibilities for errors, omissions or contradictory information contained in this book. The author and publisher make no representation or warranties with respect to the accuracy, applicability, fitness, or completeness of the contents of this book. The information contained in this book is strictly for educational purposes. The author and publisher do not warrant the performance, effectiveness or applicability of any information or sites listed or linked to in this book. All references and links are for information purposes only and are not warranted for content, accuracy or any other implied or explicit purpose. Results from using any information in this book will be totally dependent on individual circumstances and factors beyond the control of the author. The author's results may vary from your results. This book is not intended as legal, health, or diet advice. The reader of this publication assumes all responsibility for the use of these materials and information. Some links in this document may earn the publisher a sales commission. The author assumes no responsibility or liability whatsoever on behalf of any purchaser or reader of these materials. Disclaimer: This book is my opinion. I am not a lawyer, I am not an accountant, so before you get started implementing any of my suggestions, you need to consult your attorney or your accountant to make legal decisions, particularly that have to do with your particular state and local government regulations.

NETBALL BASICS: HOW TO PLAY NETBALL

Kim Sundrey

I dedicate this book to every person – who has been lucky enough to have their lives touched by the joy, excitement and sheer buzz of netball...

Contents

1. Netball: An Introduction
2. Basic Netball Equipment
3. How to Choose Netball Shoes
4. Netball Shooting Tips and Techniques
5. Top Attacking Skills and Techniques
6. Netball Shooters Defensive Tips
7. Improving Your Basic Skills
8. A Social Game
9. Boosting Your Health
10. Give It a Try

Netball:
An Introduction

Netball was first played in the United States in 1895.

It was known as a lady's version of basketball, which was invented a few years before netball.

At that time, women's clothing wasn't really practical and made playing basketball particularly awkward, which was why some amendments were made, thus forming the game of netball we know today.

These days, netball is played by people from all parts of the world.

However, the sport is most commonly associated with New Zealand, Australia, the West Indies and Sri Lanka.

As people become increasingly worried about their unhealthy lifestyles, interest in fun and challenging sports continue to increase.

People are now becoming more image conscious even at a young age and they're becoming more concerned about their weight.

Rather than taking dieting to an extreme level, which is just as unhealthy as leading a sedentary life, more people are looking for healthier ways of maintaining their weight.

And because it's important to encourage a healthy lifestyle from a young age, many schools are now offering netball as part of their physical education program.

It's now common for school gym supply rooms to have netball equipment, since the sport is considered as both fun and fashionable.

Community

Outside school campuses, netball lessons are also being offered in gyms and health clubs.

Even local communities are becoming more aware that there aren't as many healthy activities for the young as there should be.

This awareness has led to an increasing fear that teenagers may develop antisocial behaviours as a result of hanging around without much physical exercise, which may be one of the reasons why youth clubs are now offering netball lessons as a possible solution.

Get fit

Netball is indeed an exciting way to keep in shape and it's the kind of sport that offers great fun for people regardless of their age.

Regardless of why you've decided to learn how to play netball, though, you always need to remember that leading an active and healthy lifestyle doesn't have to be boring. It can and should, in fact, be a lot of fun.

If you're currently going through a rigid dieting program, it may be difficult for you to picture leading a healthy lifestyle as fun, but once you start exercising by playing netball, you'll realise how this sport can lift your spirits and help you keep fit at the same time.

Getting Started in Netball

Netball is a fast-paced and thrilling game, but before you start playing it, you'll need to take the time to study its basic rules and learn how to play the game.

- Your main goal in the sport of netball is to score as many goals as possible by shooting the ball into your opponent's post.

- Since the game can be played by people of all age groups, there are several different sizes of balls for you to choose from. Junior players aged 8-10 years old generally play with a size 4 ball, while senior players use size 5 balls.

- The balls also come in different weights. Heavier balls are generally used for practicing passes because it strengthens a player's wrists and helps improve your quickness and passing distance.

- The goal posts are among the most crucial pieces of equipment in netball. One goal post is placed at each end of the netball court and the goal rings and nets are attached at the top of these posts. The poles come in two different sizes:

- The juniors pole, which is 2.4 metres high and the seniors pole, which is 3.05 metres high.

  Being a team sport, one of the most important abilities you need to develop in netball is your passing skills.

- There are seven players in each netball team and each player is restricted to a certain part of the court. A special identification mark is placed on the uniform of each player to indicate his position. This mark is normally referred to as a bib.

- Bibs are also among the most important pieces of netball equipment. They help referees and spectators identify which players are holding which positions.

  This also makes it easier for referees to determine if certain players have strayed from their designated positions. Bibs are typically made from breathable fabric and each netball team needs to have its own bib colour.

Bibs also have specific labels that help identify each of the players even from a distance.

- Other pieces of equipment that are necessary for playing netball are protective shorts, netball shoes, and personal training gear.

The good thing is that there are many sports stores that sell these items and some of these stores even offer the items for sale on their own websites.

This means you can easily search for any equipment you need online and buy whatever you need without having to leave the comforts of your own home.

The items can be shipped and delivered right to your doorstep without any hassles! And you can start looking forward to becoming fitter and healthier while having lots of fun.

The Details

- The netball court is 100ft by 50ft in dimension.

- A netball match typically lasts for an hour, which is divided into four 15-minute quarters.
- The primary aim of the game is to score as many goals as possible by shooting the ball into the opponent's goal, which is a metal hoop attached to a metal pole.

- At the end of the 60 minutes game time, the team with the most number of goals is declared the winner of the match.

Netball is typically played by seven players on each team, covering the following positions:

- Goalkeeper
- Goal Defender
- Goal Attacker
- Goal Shooter
- Wing Defender
- Wing Attacker
- Centre

The players can switch positions throughout the match, with players being allowed to make the switch at the end of every quarter or in the event of an injury substitution.

- The court is divided into three sections, with a shooting area enclosed in a semi-circle at each end of the court.
- The movements of each player are restricted to a particular area on the court.
- The goalkeeper is allowed to move only within their team's semi-circle as well as within their defensive third.
- The goal defender can move within their team's semi-circle, defensive third, and the court's middle third.
- The goal attacker is allowed to move within the middle third of the court, the opponent's third, and the opponent's semi-circle.
- The goal shooter can move within the opponent's third and semi-circle.

- The wing defender can move only within their team's defensive third and the court's middle third.

- The wing attacker can move within the court's middle third and the opponent's defensive third.
- The centre is allowed to move within all three thirds of the court, but not within the semi-circles.

  NOTE: You should also take note that the ball cannot be thrown directly from the first to the last third of the court.

- A player is allowed to throw the ball only as far as two-thirds away at a time. Players are also prohibited from travelling with the ball.

  This means that when the ball is in your possession, you should be able to release it within three seconds, at which point it should come into contact with the ground or be passed to another player.

- There are two umpires who govern a netball game, one on the court area and one on the sidelines.

- Netball is governed by the International Federation of Netball Associations (IFNA), which is based in Manchester, England. There are currently three international netball competitions: The World Series, the World Netball Championships, and the Olympics.

Australia currently holds the title of world netball champion. While the sport is played in more than 80 countries all over the world, it's most popular in Australia, New Zealand, and the United Kingdom.

Each of these countries has its own Superleague, with the United Kingdom's championship title currently being held by the Hertfordshire Mavericks.

Basic Netball Equipment

As you start learning how to play netball, you naturally take the time to learn about its rules.

You also take the time to study the different moves, positions, and restrictions associated with the game.

Other than that, you also need to learn what basic netball equipment you need to acquire so you can practice the game at home or introduce it to your family and friends.

The basic netball equipment you need to acquire is:

- **The ball**

    The ball is a bit softer and lighter than a basketball, as it's meant to encourage a fast-paced game even if players aren't allowed to run with the ball.

    There are balls available for indoor or outdoor use as well as balls that can be used for both. Size 4 balls are typically used by junior players whereas size 5 balls are used by senior players.

    For home practice, a training ball may suffice.

But, for purposes of a school or club team, several training balls may be needed along with at least two match-quality balls that can be used in competitive games.

- **Post**

    For the netball post, you can choose between a free-standing post that can be wheeled away when not in use and a post that can be screwed into a socket.

    The standard height of a netball post is ten feet, but it typically has two lower settings for junior players and toddlers.

    If you don't have enough room at home for regulation-sized posts, then you can choose from any of the garden-style sets currently being sold. You can choose between posts that separate into sections and posts that can be mounted on a wall.

    Wall-mounted posts are especially useful to children, who can use the wall as a backboard.

- **Bib**

    Another piece of equipment netball players need is the netball bib, which is basically a Velcro patch where the position letters of each player are printed.

    This is important because each player is only allowed to operate within certain parts of the netball court and the bib will help determine if any player has violated these restrictions.

    Bibs are typically sold in sets of seven (one for each player in the team) and some netball uniforms even come with their own set of bibs.

    There are also reversible bibs available, which make it easy for teams to switch bibs when they play at home or away.

- **Cones**

    Training equipment such as cones may also come in handy, since netball has very specific rules and players are required to follow very strict patterns so as not to get penalised.

It's therefore wise to practice your footwork with the use of training cones that can help enhance your ability to weave, throw, and catch.

- **Shoes**

    Of course, you'll also need a good pair of shoes that are specifically designed for the sport. These shoes are designed such that they're able to withstand the strain associated with netball.

    Take note that there are shoes designed for indoor or outdoor use as well as shoes that can be worn for both.

- **Clothing**

    Finally, you'll need the appropriate clothing for playing netball.

    For training purposes, you'll need tracksuits and perhaps base layers for comfort and improved performance.

When you buy a netball kit, it'll typically include a skirt and blouse with Lycra underpants. These days, however, dresses and shorts have become more popular.

Because netball isn't a full-contact sport, players aren't required to wear head gear.

You can, in fact, be fouled simply for leaning into an opponent.

It's easy to find an entire range of netball equipment from most good sports shops.

How to Choose
Netball Shoes

Footwork is considered as one of the most important netball skills you need to learn when playing this sport.

It therefore makes sense to wear a pair of shoes that'll provide you with both safety and comfort as you play.

Standard sports shoes or running shoes aren't going to be adequate for the specific needs of netball players.

So, if you seriously want to perform well in this sport, you'll need to get the right kind of shoes.

Here are some tips on how to choose the right netball shoes:

1. **Movement**

    You need to think about your movements during a netball game when choosing netball shoes.

    Remember that the sport requires a lot of running as well as plenty of quick stops, sudden changes in direction, and lateral movements.

The shoes you choose need to be able to support these movements.

Standard running shoes are designed only for straightforward motion, thus focusing support on the heels and toes.

For netball purposes, you need to find shoes that offer all-around support along with cushioning and maximum comfort for the sides of your feet.

2. **Stability**

   Because netball involves a lot of jumping and stop-start movements, you'll definitely need a pair of shoes that can sufficiently handle the pressure.

   As you catch the ball and pivot for a pass, you'll want to be assured that your shoes are going to support the movement and keep you well-balanced.

3. **Outsole**

   Standard running shoes are typically flexible, especially in the area right under your forefeet.

The opposite is true of netball shoes.

The outsoles of these shoes need the ability to withstand punishment by the cement or asphalt of a netball court. It therefore needs to be significantly thicker and stiffer than regular running shoes.

This is why netball shoes are often made of completely different materials than standard running shoes and a harder rubber compound.

4. **Profile**

   Netball shoes typically have shorter profiles than running shoes.

   This means they're lower to the ground in order to allow flexibility and a greater range of movement.

   And with your feet on lower platforms, the risk of rolling your ankles is greatly reduced. Netball shoes are designed to be tough and durable enough to withstand the harsh demands of the sport as well as your swift legwork.

NOTE: You may notice a lot of indoor netball players still preferring to use standard sports shoes or running shoes when playing.

This is quite alright because indoor courts are typically made of wood rather than asphalt and running shoes are generally lighter than netball shoes, which allows you to move more easily.

Of course, you'll have to choose the shoes that fit you most comfortably, regardless of whether they're running shoes or especially-designed netball shoes.

If you feel most comfortable wearing running shoes in a netball game, then so be it, as long as you're prepared to buy new shoes from time to time.

The biggest advantage of choosing netball shoes is that they're designed specifically with the game and the player in mind.

Netball Shooting
Tips and Techniques

You may already have learned to throw, catch, pivot, and block like a pro in the game of netball, but perhaps you're still having some problems with your shooting.

NOTE: Take note that the ability to shoot the ball accurately is an important skill to develop for this sport.

Of all netball playing positions only the goal attackers and goal shooters have the opportunity to score for the team and if you hold either of these positions, then you're definitely going to want a high success rate.

In the three seconds you're allowed to shoot the ball, it's important to be confident in your shooting abilities and techniques.

Here are some tips for improving your netball shooting:

1. When someone tries to block you in an attempt to shoot, you should do your best to ignore them.

    As long as the goal post is within your line of sight, there's a good chance they won't be able to intercept the shot.

2. Take note of how you stand as you prepare to shoot the ball.

    Remember that balance is essential to accurate shooting, since you need to have a stable stance in order to shoot properly.

    Height is also an important factor, since it provides an obvious advantage over shorter players. Regardless of your height, though, you'll need to stand with your feet about a shoulder-width apart when you shoot.

    You can also experiment with other shooting stances during practice to see which stance you're most comfortable with.

3. How you hold the ball is also important, as it dictates the spring, power, and spin of your shot. Make sure your stronger hand, also known as your shooting hand, is positioned behind and just under the ball.

4. You should also make sure that your fingers are bent and that the ball is cradled with your fingertips. This gives your shot extra spin and boost.

   Your other hand should offer support by cradling the side of the ball. This is also the hand you use to aim, so make sure it's pointed towards the net.

   Always remember that it's important to keep the ball well-balanced in this position as you make the shot.

5. Practice the squat, which is basically the first part of shooting. It builds up potential energy for when you release the ball and hopefully ends in a goal.

   Take note that the power of a shot comes not from your hands, but from your legs. Your arms and fingers work primarily to provide direction to the shot.

   With the ball held in position, bend your knees while keeping your back straight and holding your head high.

Remember to keep your eyes on the goal and your hands in the right position. How low you need to squat depends on your personal preference. It's therefore wise to experiment during practice.

6. Making the actual shot is where you finally release all that potential energy. Be sure to focus on the ring, particularly the back part of the ring.

    Remember as well that the shot has to come when your body is extended.

    Release the ball as your knees and arms straighten out, but remember that's not all there is to shooting the ball. As you release the ball, be sure to spin it backwards by flicking your wrist.

    This has the effect of making the ball bounce back towards you in case the ball hits the back of the ring.

7. As soon as you release the ball, be sure to follow it towards the ring. This makes it easier for you to grab that second chance in case the ball doesn't go in.

Just like everything else in sports, becoming an ace netball shooter takes a lot of practice.

Practicing netball shooting drills is probably the only real way to achieve the kind of accuracy you need to become an ace goal shooter.

Keep practicing until your shooting backspin and focus become second nature.

Top Attacking
Skills and Techniques

The attack is an extremely important move in the sport of netball.

A successful attack requires a high level of coordination, good tactical skills, and situational awareness.

The best netball players can make a successful attack simply by getting hold of the ball from practically anywhere on the court.

Other than excellent netball skills, the best attackers also have excellent timing.

Here are some of the most important skills and techniques you need to develop in order to become an effective attacker:

1. Attack Principles

There are some things that all effective attacks have in common.

For one thing, they all rely on locating and exploiting a weakness in the opponent's defence.

These attacks are also able to turn a defensive situation into an effective attacking situation.

Furthermore, an effective attack gains play initiative, which often reflects on the scoreboard.

Finally, all effective attacks are potentially demoralising for the opponent. This is what makes an effective attack the perfect recipe for a winning netball game.

Always remember that the basic element in the principles of attack is the fact that the attacker always dictates the play and the opponent is forced into a reactive and less productive form of play.

Your opponents aren't likely to score if they're too busy responding to your attacks.

2. Attack Techniques

The classic and perhaps the most lethal form of attack is a highly penetrating move that throws the opponent's defence off-balance.

Instead of being focused and coordinated, the opponent's defence is forced to scramble and become somewhat disorganised.

Most killer attacks include a long pass into an open zone, which often leads to wrong footing the opponents.

Another effective attack is one involving several players, which separates the opponent into several defensive groups.

Finally, you can execute a sudden attack from defence, which surprises and upends the field positions.

These moves generally work by making the defence work twice as hard.

You could also try to expose slow movers in the opposing team by making a few bullet-like passes.

3. Attack Development

Always make sure that your attack has both an objective and a backup. You need to develop plays such that two or three players can immediately support the attacking move.

NOTE: Take note that the effect of adequate support triples the effectiveness of the attack.

Your opponent's defence will naturally try to shut down your attack.

When your support players receive the ball, the opponents will be forced to reposition and if they fail to cover the support, then the attack is successful.

Such fast and multi-faceted attacks can effectively wear down even a very good defence. So, how do you become a good attacker?

You become a good attacker by developing excellent situational awareness, becoming a good judge of distance and space, developing agility and quickness, and by getting instant support from your teammates who recognise your attacking move.

Attack training may make you breathless, but it'll definitely pay off in the long run.

A good attack is not only beautiful to watch, but it also demonstrates what a truly skilled netball player can do.

Shooters Defensive Tips

Some netball players are simply amazing.

They're extremely agile, unbelievably fast, have the ability to jump high, have very quick hands, can effectively fake a pass, shoot accurately, and make use of a wide variety of moves.

And as if that's not enough, these players are also quite brilliant at putting pressure on their opponents down the court.

In order to become this kind of amazingly great all-around netball player, you'll also need to learn how to defend, of course.

In fact, you'll want to develop the ability of becoming a real pest to your opponent.

Full-court defence is often the best way to pressure your opponents in a netball game.

This means all seven players on your team should have each other covered and you should each be relentless in attempting to intercept passes and put pressure on the player who has the ball.

Experts agree that it's so much easier to score a goal in netball if you work the ball down the court in about three to four passes.

By making the defenders work extra hard at bringing the ball down the court, you're practically forcing your team to be patient and more often than not, this results in an error on the part of your opponent such as a bad pass, a spilled ball, or a held ball.

If the ball is in your opponent's hands and you're in a shooting or attacking position, then your job basically the same as the rest of your team, which is to do your best to get the ball back into your possession.

Here are a few tips to help you become a better defender:

1. Learn how to accurately estimate the distance of three feet. Once you've learned to do this, jump back three feet the moment the player you're guarding receives a pass and then put your hands up immediately in order to pressure the next pass.

2. Once your opponent has passed the ball, take a step forward immediately to try blocking their next drive.

3. Keep the communication lines open within the team. If your player drives to one direction and you know you can't reach the pass, then yell for your teammate to try intercepting it instead.

   Constantly yelling directions to your teammates can also serve to distract your opponent and add to the pressure.

4. If you hold the position of goal attacker, then you should defend both two thirds and you should never slack off in the goal third!

   If your opponent makes a centre pass, be sure to defend your team's goal defender tightly.

5. Develop the ability to switch from attacking to defensive mode quickly.

In case you throw a bad pass, you need to be able to recover quickly and work on getting the ball back or shutting down the opponent's play.

Always remember that fitness counts a lot in netball. For one thing, it takes a high fitness level to constantly put pressure on your opponent.

Concentrating on getting the ball back also helps develop your confidence in netball shooting.

In case you miss a shot, you can set your heart on immediately getting the ball back, thus preventing you from dwelling on the missed shot.

Improving Your Basic Skills

Skills training for any sport is necessarily founded on the basics and the best sporting technique has to do with developing some basic skills.

In the sport of netball, the primary skills you need to learn and master are:

- Ball handling
- Movement

The abilities you need to develop to compliment these are:

- Balance
- Coordination
- Good reflexes
- Quick responses

In order to achieve all these, you'll need to do more than practice.

In fact, effective netball training requires systematic management so you can meet high standards. This involves identifying your weak points and focusing your training on strengthening those points. This way, skills gaps can be effectively filled.

Muscle groups

Basic netball skills training cover the development of your muscle groups that are primarily involved in the sport.

Some of the skill sets in basic netball training are:

- Passing and movement - where you learn how to handle the ball while moving
- Basic speed and accuracy - where you're required to pass the ball at a sprint.
- Development speed and accuracy - where four players return the passes to feeders.

These fundamental game skills soon become among your most reliable reflexes. And these sets not only build your basic skills, but also your confidence, which is essential during a game.

Differences

Even for the best netball players, skill development is rarely consistent. One player may be an excellent passer, but may struggle with receiving. There are also great defenders who get lost in attacking moves.

In basic netball training, each player is typically given a score for each skill, with ten being the highest possible score. The scores will show which areas a player needs to put some extra focus on.

Your training will then place more emphasis on the areas wherein you show low scores. This works well for developing you into a better-skilled, all-around player.

Stamina

The activities you're required to do in netball all require high stamina and the level of agility you develop depends largely on your fitness level. This is why netball training needs to combine skills training with fitness training.

Balance training is particularly important, since good balance helps ensure proper muscle group action, which reduces fatigue and strain. Training for netball can be likened to training for a marathon. You need to increase your stamina in order to produce more stamina.

However, you should also practice good judgement when you train for stamina because doing too much too soon can do more harm than good. The results of your training also need to be measured consistently and you should refrain from making allowances for performance that isn't really up to scratch or anything that shows some serious weaknesses.

The standards you set for yourself should also be consistent.

Always remember that a substandard player is and will always be a liability to the team.

There should be no confusion about what's good enough and what falls short.

With a consistent set of standards, all players on the team will know what's expected of them and work hard towards their goal.

A Social Game

In this day and age, technology has taken over our lives so much that many people's idea of socialising no longer involves face-to-face interaction, but is often limited to the online environment.

While the ability to communicate with people from all over the world is indeed attractive, it can also limit your prospects for social interaction within a local base. If you want to interact with people within your own locality or if you want to participate in a fun and energetic activity with like-minded individuals, then it's good to know that there are still some real opportunities offered by such activities as mixed netball.

In fact, this game is one of the most popular activities in Australia because it encourages social interaction outside the realm of technology.

Get to know people

The social opportunities offered by netball provide any person with the chance to get to know other people in an entirely new environment where personal interaction is not only encouraged, but also greatly supported.

When you join a group that frequently participates in netball games, you get the opportunity to interact with people on a regular basis, which lays the foundation for developing friendships and solid social connections.

Mixed netball is played by small teams that are generally in continued motion and constantly interact with each other in the pursuit of their individual and team goals.

The activity itself helps eliminate any awkwardness team members may feel at first as they meet new people. It also helps begin the intricate process of building new and lasting friendships.

New relationship

While netball offers several advantages to the individual who wants to build local social networks, there are just as many wonderful opportunities in this sport for groups looking to interact outside traditional outlets.

Regardless of whether you're planning to join an existing team or building one of your own, the experience you gain with netball allows you to interact with other people regularly.

Other than the opportunity for social interaction, mixed netball also allows you to discover new opportunities for health enhancement as you go through the energetic movements associated with the game.

The sport also provides you with new avenues for entertainment as you start building relationships with your teammates and even with opposing teams.

Boosting your health

If you want to live a long life, then it's essential for you to maintain your health.

And while many people claim to take their health seriously, the reality is that their busy schedules often make it difficult for them to take advantage of some very good opportunities for improving or maintaining their overall health.

As more and more people embrace sedentary lifestyles and take advantage of the convenience offered by fast food services, the overall health of the population quickly deteriorates.

If you're currently in a situation where you want to improve your overall health, but you don't really want to go through boring and repetitive exercises, then you may want to consider getting engaged in netball.

For someone who's trying to find a way of improving overall health, netball's upbeat pace may just be the perfect and most satisfying solution.

One of the most common reasons why people can't stick to an exercise program is that they get bored with it after some time.

The atmosphere created by mixed netball, where each team has the goal of winning makes the activity extremely entertaining and takes away the boredom commonly associated with exercise.

With netball, you get an excellent aerobic workout without ever becoming bored.

Mental fitness

When you start looking for ways of improving your overall health, you're likely to consider diet and exercise.

While a good combination of diet and exercise can indeed improve your physical health, it may not always take into account your mental health.

With a sport like netball, however, you'll realise that it not only challenges you physically, but also mentally as you work on the different strategies and techniques that'll help you win the game.

Traditional exercises that involve minimal cardio and repetitive movements may not really do much for your mental health, but the constant motion and high participation levels required in netball forces you to challenge yourself intellectually.

As a result, your mental health will surely be stimulated and significantly improved.

Diet

Netball is a fast-paced game that requires a certain discipline and that discipline extends to your diet.

As you already know, food serves as your body's fuel, which means that it's extremely important for your body to function as it should.

While your normal diet may get you through a single game each week, you're going to have to exert more effort if you want to get the most out of your physical capabilities.

And if you train for netball several times each week and then play more than once a week, then nutrition will definitely play a crucial role in improving your game.

Not only will eating the right kinds of food at the right times each day prepare your body for the game, but it will also aid your muscles in recovery.

Furthermore, being in control of your diet will not only get you in fighting form for the game, but will also ensure you have enough energy for your daily routines.

Planning

The best way to control your diet is to plan your meals on a weekly basis.

It's often a good idea to cook a big batch of food and then divide it into the number of meals you'll be taking for the next few days.

This way, you can simply heat up a healthy meal whenever you come home from a netball game or training session.

This is also an excellent way of avoiding junk food, which people typically munch on right after some heavy physical exertion.

You may also want to reorganise your daily schedules such that you have your main meal during the day or prepare it during the day so you can eat it as soon as you get home from a game or from training.

Cook

To achieve your goal of maintaining a healthy diet, it's essential that you know how to cook.

If nobody in your household knows how to cook, then it could be a good idea to consult a dietician or sports nutritionist to help you out.

Alternatively, you can start learning how to cook with the help of a healthy recipe book, which you can easily find at your local bookstore or online.

NOTE: Remember that controlling your diet doesn't necessarily mean you can't snack in between meals.

In fact, snacking can keep your metabolism high.

What's important is for you to be careful about what you snack on.

Slow energy-releasing foods like fruits are your best choices and you need to keep away from chocolate bars.

Proper pre-game nutrition is very important for having enough stamina and energy for netball.

A carbohydrate-rich and low-fat meal is ideal two to three hours prior to a game, as it will provide you with plenty of slow-burning energy that's sure to get you through every single quarter of the game.

It's important for you to make sure you have enough fluid in your body before, during, and after the game.

And while it's easy to remember to drink water before and after the game, many players take hydration for granted during the game.

Be sure to have a water bottle handy and take a sip in between quarters and during timeouts so you don't get dehydrated.

Of course, you should also take care of your body right after a game. Go for fruit or carbohydrate-rich food such as sandwiches and always remember that what you eat immediately after a game directly impacts your body, which is why you need to be very careful.

Your body needs nutrition in order to perform and it needs the right kind of nutrition in order to perform at optimum levels.

Therefore, being in control of your diet is just as important in netball as getting adequate training.

So go on, give it a try

Now you know about the basics of netball why not give it a try?

People who start netball often become addicted to this high-energy sport.

Here are some of the best reasons to play:

- Start to play at any age
- Both males and females can play
- Simple, easy to learn rules
- Inexpensive to get started
- Great for your health.

So get inspired and try netball today.

Printed in Great Britain
by Amazon